T0072183

THE
SHAPE
OF
REGRET

THE SHAPE OF REGRET

POEMS BY
HERBERT WOODWARD MARTIN

WAYNE STATE UNIVERSITY PRESS
Detroit

© 2019 by Herbert Woodward Martin. All rights reserved.
No part of this book may be reproduced without formal permission.

ISBN 978-0-8143-4724-9 (paperback); ISBN 978-0-8143-4725-6 (ebook)

Library of Congress Control Number: 2019944714

Wayne State University Press
Leonard N. Simons Building
4809 Woodward Avenue
Detroit, Michigan 48201-1309
Visit us online at wsupress.wayne.edu

for
Arthur and Ruth Efron
Frank and Kathleen Surico

Contents

Acknowledgments

Some of these poems had their births in the following journals and little magazines:

Common Threads: "Fish Story," "Unknown"
House Organ: "Toccata, "Regret," "Janet Jackson's Nipple"
HQ Poetry Magazine: "Contemplations on Snow"
Kerf: "Three Poems After Lucille Clifton," "Velazquez's Painting of Maria Teresa," "A Time for Bees"
Notre Dame Review: "Enigma: The Unanswered Question," "Villanelle for an Auspicious
Occasion," "Translucent Fish Scales," "Twelve Black Crows"
Ocho: "After William Carlos Williams' "The Red Wheelbarrow"
Plainsongs: "Mutability"
Poems for Walt Whitman (2019): "After Walt Whitman"
Pouch: "Appraising"
Stand: "A Deft Old Man," "Reading an Old Poetry Issue," "Untitled #2"
The Caribbean Writer: "The Warning," "Kitchen Activity"

I owe Joel Lipman a world of honor and appreciation because he encouraged me to take a hard look at an overblown manuscript. We all need an Ezra Pound. He was mine! And I am grateful.

THREE
MUSICIANS

Enigma: The Unanswered Question

After Charles Ives

Every morning you come into the kitchen looking desperate.
I say: *eat something; take something from the bowl on the table*
or that's fresh in the refrigerator or that's prepared in the cabinet,
but you never listen to me. Why? Aren't you hungry? Aren't you
fierce for something that will sustain you? Don't you need food
like the rest of us who call ourselves humans? You always seem
to be looking past the food to something else that I never see.
What is it that commands your attention outside the window,
in the air beyond this room, away from this house? Is it something,
in some hidden quarter of the city, or in the last row of the farm
where you tilled most of the day? What is it? Does it reside near
the edge of the town river, at the railroad tracks where the (419)
is always on time, and goes bum-ble, bum-ble, bum-ble, until
every last car has crossed over the city line and headed off into
the distance seeking that special unknown destination.
Every morning each citizen yawns and wonders the same thing
before falling back to sleep. What is it they ask? Why won't you
tell them the answer? Even the cat pauses now and then
before an answer can be detected.

An English Street Vendor

Edith Sitwell
does she sit well
with her classical
well-trained mind?

Yes, Dame Sitwell
quite well sits well
on her pinnacle
far from hell.

There she nourishes,
and she flourishes
with her cry:
Good poems to sell.

Five Finger Exercise

For Bradley

fingers are appendages of compassion,
the face withers from such a touch.
even death pauses and is attentive,
and men look on with a gentle quietness,
while women dress themselves in
mournful grief, and the children wear
forgetful noises. nature is a wizard
that entertains, curious wonder is the
mathematical scientist with a rational
experiment that advises advantage and
prayer which is the miracle of legislative
words that we have weighed when
we have to measure chance against truth.

Reading the Eyes of My Masters

THREE NEW LINES FOR HART CRANE
(1899–1932)

Large fish feast in substantive waters;
Sea grass wavers around a vest of ribs.
I begin to imagine the rule of electricity.

CONTEMPLATIONS ON SNOW

In memory of Wallace Stevens

I
Midnight has dreams of snow that filled the driveway, said the son.
Then let Midnight remove the snow, said the mother.
Some birds are not happy with the snow, observed the wife.
Fresh snow frustrates everyone it comes in contact with;
it is an ancient falling that marries itself to tree, the husband
      acknowledges.
In the distance, a neighbor listens to the wind's mediation.
Further along the avenue music comes from the piano teacher's
      house,
her student struggles with the rhythms of a Beethoven sonata;
the melodies were pieces of moonlight that fell centuries ago.
Snow anticipates large silences,
it approaches an evening with its own resonance.
Spring will come with its own sentences of love
uttered from the deepest parts of the night.
The student follows his alert fingers when the music is accurate;
he remains at the piano; his fingers are a willing testament.

II
A candle burns in a window;
a crazy quilt hinders all breezes;
the night is a thunderous presence;
a lantern stands on a shelf, resting.

III
Give me a broom to sweep away
the dust of annoyance;
below the slats of the floor

there is a cavity for a runaway
to rest in sleep.
Still hounds seek his scent,
his every hesitant turn;
they will seek him out.
What guides them to be so hungry?
What is it that urges them forward?

IV
When a slave escapes
he wraps himself in
the dusk of evening;
he is unable to weep
away the fears of shadows;
he has anchored himself
in his forefather's truths;
they disappeared a long time ago;
they are long gone, now.

After William Carlos Williams' "The Red Wheelbarrow"

So much depends
upon
a penis snaking
its way
through the luscious walls
of a
vagina whose environs
demand
ascending and descending
pleasures
which can be derived
from no
other action and no
other
root source and
cannot
be delivered in any
other
fashion, nor in any
other
pleasurable form.

DEAR BILL

After William Carlos Williams

This is just to say
that hurricane Ike
denuded the Oak
and White Birch
trees that stood on
both sides of our
house; the bark
and leaves and
limbs decapitated,
blossoms laid waste
on the city's best
piece of landscape
which forced me
to abandon all the
foods I had horded
for the future.
In all the items
I had saved, there
was not one single
piece of fresh fruit,
and certainly, no plums.

AFTER WALT WHITMAN

What is lightning?
    my granddaughter asks.
I do not know,
    is what I tell her.
Is it a tributary,
    a river falling from the sky?
Is it the finger of God,
    listening to the fears of the flesh?
What are acts of insubordination?
    Are they opening the gates of choice?
Has the heart always been innocent?
    Yes, it has always been a seeker of resonance,
just as one generation departs from another.
    Such an act is not a dismissive handshake,
it is not a handkerchief to blow the nose upon,
    nor a thread to wipe away perspiration.
These are my observations, Granddaughter!

On Reading Lucille Clifton's "Homage to My Hips"

I am here to praise ungainly women
the ones with large pork chop hips
that sway with the motion of the earth
and with the intrigue of wind and shadows
alternately moving and bending with the
leaves on the vines, and subsequently to
tickle the hipbone which maintains that
heavy abundance which allows women
to dance on the arms of the sun or to
swing so low that they hear the earth cry out:
Choose me: take me home!

My mother had similar hips;
they beckoned when she encountered
men of her choosing:
their eyes appreciated what they saw.
All men of color say they must pay
strict attention when they receive
such personal invitations.

THREE POEMS

After Lucille Clifton

At the drop of a hat, stop and ask for directions.
My reticent family pretends to be too shy to ask,
too embarrassed to inquire; I forge ahead because
I know that there are dangers up ahead that veer
into nothing; I also know that there are strangers
up ahead who possess answers.

Once, we were lost in Western Hungary, in the
deepest and darkest kind of loneliness and a hand
knocked on the window of our car and pointed to
the map on my wife's lap. His finger traced its way
from his city to our city while our eyes followed
faithfully. I have always been grateful for the
knowledge others have in their possession.

APOLOGY

The day is filled
with random apologies,
socially polite greetings,
which we offer to white
people as real substance,
testifying who we truly are,
because they are given to
thinking, faultily, that we are
miserable enough not to know
how to apologize for the painful
afflictions their fathers cast upon
our fathers. But we are dressed
in truth and wear it faithfully.

MUTABILITY

Sometimes I sprinkle salt
on a peach or a plum and
a luscious sweetness
attaches itself to the flesh
of the fruit, and all the
sourness of what I have
begun to ingest disappears.

On Reading Wendell Berry's Sabbaths

I
Wander in pristine darkness,
encounter a rhythm,
you will not see a feather moving
nor hear a thrush's murmur;
still, something will
mock your innocence

II
Travel in shade or sun
hugged by a timeless wind
be welcome in resolute darkness;
your alert senses will prevent you
from falling into dangerous ravines

III
The woods, like you, are becoming hoary;
they are a generation away from slavery,
one league from the local river,
where nightly escape was possible,
where you often entertained earthly labors
that made you desire more

Variations on Some Index Phrases
Borrowed from Kenneth Rexroth

A sad morning,
no escape,
no forgetting;
the shadow you
cast is a memory
to be embraced,
tightly,
as your hands
turn pale.

In a shady park,
the month's great heat
passes through
the evening's intensity,
and we sit and eat at last.

We learn to sleep together,
we lie under a sheet
of the callow moon.
In a green meadow,
slowly,
we become one.

Nature and the Bones of Things

A Deaf Old Man

1
The old man was deaf;
he had no ear for music
no tongue to pronounce
the residue of lyrics,
no breath in his lungs to
reveal the mysteries of life.

2
A black crow spits out white fog.
It covers the wholesome morning.
In the east a diseased cloud approaches.

3
Night descends rapidly.
Heat resonates in the hearth.
The day's work has exhausted
the old man and woman who
doze on the couch holding
affection in each other's hand.

4
The white headlights smile
the boulevard divides the
neighborhood's mediocre and poor.
Speed acknowledges shadows;
the red taillights wink.

5
The heart of a body lies in a roadside ditch;
it ceased beating days ago.

The local corner will access and tell us
several days from now the how and why.
Until then, only the wind knows the true answer.

6

The rain falls in sweet waves;
the air between the droplets remains fresh.
The old woman is renewed
by the feel of oxygen in her lungs.

7

The fire in the hearth has died;
cinders, ash and charred wood remain.
The soot of the hearth smells fresh
when the wind sighs down the chimney.

8

The green forsythia leaves are surrounded
by all the activity of white blooms;
a glaze of soundless snow fell the day before.

9

The brush of wind bruises the pine needles;
the sap sticks to my imaginary hands,
tries to reattach the spindle's leaves;
spring rains will relish them falling again.

10

The strength of light rests upon the skin.
The tongue tastes the slight chill of wind,
the eyes recognize brief acquaintances
because of the sunlight.

11

The heart is a radical organ;
pulse is the native offspring;
fingers imprison the residue of blood.

12

The trees have long black branches;
men and women and children are
similar extensions, ways of seeing;
the leaves are the eyes of God.

WEB

A unique white spider,
its web ordinary,
articulate predatory,
dust trapped in its sphere.
This web hangs green
ivy and sunlight,
it crawls between
cement holding
bricks together
dominates whatever
it touches.
A fool-hearted bee
seeks nectar and
finds itself restrained
like the dead Monarch
whose remains should
have been an alert warning
had it been paying strict
attention, but like Icarus,
it overlooked the obvious,
found itself prisoner
and feast to death.

A Time for Bees

It was a time for bees,
a gathering of pollen,
a dance of honey,
The backyard was
a jungle of wild
winged things attacking
and spreading havoc
from blossom to blossom.
Witness the quiet activity,
petal to flower, stem to stalk,
the sad leavings of love,
a rock thrown against the night,
a violent interruption of lovemaking,
that excellent moment when
terror knocks and whispers:
May I come in?

QUESTION AND ANSWER

So that poem you wrote is about your
Uncle Jaybird?
Yes!
No wonder his son was so unstable.
We do what we can.
Maybe we should do more than we are able.
All we knew is what we know now:

Somebody back then was Judge and Jury.
Somebody was an anonymous accuser.
The rest were irate citizens
acting as if they understood
what Justice truly was or meant.
Our family were the incidental bystanders;
that is what we did;
that is all we could do.

Keeping Faith with Silence

An old man can walk any distance he desires on his own
farm speaking to himself and answering if he chooses, and
acknowledging the answers pulsing the blood through his veins.
He keeps sacred confidence.

The elements do not promise nor persuade nor argue. They are
what actions are and what is held in nature's hand. We are at
the mercy of circumstance. That is why we travel out in the deep
forty where nothing confronts or contradicts.

An old woman demonstrates her authority in the open purse of
cool air. Her voice dissolves as soon as it touches air, leaving no
trace or whiff of evidence. Old women learn quietly from books.
It is the beginning of their eighth and final decade.

So, we are told, that men and women know who, what, when,
where, and why they are committed to never say anything they
did not want repeated. In the final dog days of their lives they
kept faith with their tongues.

Death is a crease in time,
it is forced to hesitate,
stop, and hang helplessly
on a precipice where we
weep over hesitancy and
failed accomplishments.
A mosquito arrives,
it is an unwelcomed guest,
still, it seats itself at table
and imbibes in the wealth of
bread and blood which
sustains him as if he
was attending church.

TWELVE BLACK CROWS

for: Kenneth Warren

Twelve black crows in mourning
black wings on the branch of a tree;
picture this scene from a kitchen window.
White squirrels in dead blades of grass
scurrying about, gathering what must
be stored, a necessary day of laborers,
hungering for a daily wage.
Old men and women drenched in
heavy black sweat, fortified from
a day's work of longing,
where sages seek two or more
grandchildren to advise who are
filled with questions about desperate work.
They, who always seem wary, know that
there will never be enough time to accomplish
what is abundantly lacking in the approaching
winters, in spite of row on row of black wings
streaking through dry fields, which were seeded by
farmers on the land, and watered by the many
itinerant hands that help move one another toward
a fruition which is not only demanded but
necessary if one is to breathe the air freely,
with accomplished joy.

TRANSLUCENT FISH SCALES

A dark fish rises
beyond wondrous
expectations, for water
always gives way to light
or to a fisherman's bait,
like a prophet's staff
that heralds skeletons
from ships, from the hull
of bows and rare imagination.
Time observes long enough
to see memory marked in the
shells of high seas, the striations
in sand beds growing into
calcified mountains,
into memories that have mermaids
singing their histories.
Galapagos turtles
crawl out of engendering mud
of spectacular possibilities with all
the first greys of winter.

BLUE

for: Guy Parsons

The language we use and the effort with which we buttress
that language makes us seem bright and fresh like new
blooming marigolds, those flowers which look like morning
suns spangling a rainbow of light with dark colors deeper
than blood. I would like to take the same flight as a bluebird,
imperial blue night, singing all the way to New Orleans, because
blue is a surer and tender sadness that will never spill over the
borders into Louisiana, nor will it rise like the fluff of biscuits or
dandelions giving shape to the wind. This blue was Eighteenth
Century and began and ended with a kind of gallantry that stops
you in your steps, imprisoning you in amber like a bumble bee
stalled in stasis waiting for lightening to strike the stone and
scatter this blue into the stars of all those who have never been
nor will ever be imagined, for I know, in the end, my blue is
grounded and surrounded by gravity.

Appraising

for: George and Jan

My mother was undeniably an amazing beauty herself; given
the opportune chance she might have astounded herself on
the celluloid screen with dreams and fantasies built all around
her, but she chose otherwise, and in the wake, left me a parcel
with photographs and a signed letter, which was later to be
discovered and passed on to the antique appraiser of our lives.
She, no doubt, hoped he would have extraordinary news about
the considered fortune that could come my way, unexpectedly.
In the course of this evaluation, he tells me I will not become
a newly minted millionaire, but he assures me of a million
memories. The letter and photos are all signed by the screen
legend's mother and the myth of her dashing blonde hair was
all concocted by The Movie Studios to make her presence a vast
and memorable one on the silver screen. Her name was Jean
Harlow, and at the moment the letter was written, she was dying
from the chemicals the movie scions had fed her to make her
and her hair a lasting vision of desire. Her mother had signed
the letter and the photograph affectionately, *Jean Harlow*, and
although what I possessed was clearly a forgery, I still had in my
hands sure memories of a time and presence addressed to my
mother who had an astounding beauty all her own.

FAMILIARS

GETTING OUT OF THE SHOWER

for: Mac Hammond

I shall always remember the time when one of your colleagues
    said to me:
I surrendered to conquered eyes; it was too late to achieve;
I relinquished my determined vision.
It was then, at that moment, I remembered a black man's
    thought from long ago.
It is never too late to win the prize
no use retiring until death makes his presence known,
and even then, there is one more moment, a single gesture to be
    made,
a breath to be taken, that will spur you across dignity's goal
with all your intentions intact.
It is then that you realize the goal was yours all along.

TOCCATA

for: Carole Berge

I hear my sister singing in her room,
the melodies tell me she has loosed
her dark hair and soon will immerse
herself in a warm and enveloping bath
in preparation for the coming day.
When the sun has fully risen,
she will newly compete and I shall
learn what song she has been
singing in her room.

MERCEDES CAR LICENSE: 788 LTV75

In memory of a princess

Love in a pile of rubble,
a rash of mellifluous sadness,
the sound of turbulent desire
blooming upwards,
breathing loss,
energy rolling backwards upon itself:
the ritual of love,
the sound of metal crushing,
the smell of an infection,
the balance of silk upon silk,
a Sunday morning body
like the one discovered
next to Wallace Stevens'
concupiscent curds
all dry and civil, like words
in a communion of syllables.

Velazquez's Painting of Maria Teresa

has Iberian eyes,
royal lasers,
black wounds
born to exorcise
translucent colors
from men's hearts.
The rivulets of her hair
falls beneath
a phlegmatic veneer.
Her face is covered with
a brocade of Spanish sheen.

A Deadly Game

A young black boy
age 13 joins his
white friends in
a game of
bricks and walls.
The white boys
smile and prepare
to execute his
blackness.
They restrain
his arms,
place him on
a wooden
scaffold called for
lynching.

They stand at a respectful distance.
They wait for him to cleverly die;
then they will all go home, laughing.

MISSISSIPPI POPLARS

A grey moss hangs from several Mississippi trees,
it wafts in an evening breeze
ghosts without purpose
flayed skin without being.
Where have these ancestors gone?
Who claims legal right to their spirits?
Time tells us nothing.
Circumstance quiets the air.
How steadily they move, the wild branches,
the remnants that hang there.

A Meditation

My heart ceases to beat
the past moments
when experience goaded
my pulse and blood
to travel the route
my arteries and veins took.
No one has declared
which direction is true,
but I must tell you, my body
loves north and south.
Neither Harriet nor Sojourner
are here to direct my faltering
feet toward freedom.
No John Brown nor John Henry
to readily strike a righteous blow
or drive steel into the ground for liberty.

EXTRACTED FROM THE LUNGS

Each time I venture into the backyard,
my granddaughter uses the occasion
to announce how happy the country's
flag seems to be, joyfully in the next
yard when the wind moves its folds
and colors and its stars in unimaginable
ripples, and how sad its mood turns
when the wind pauses to take a rest.
I am amazed that the lungs of the sky
are always filled with air.

Note from a Chinese E-Mail

I
O, rare mysterious menu:
mushrooms from the belly of explosive fish,
white rice in a blue bowl.

II
O, mysterious food that
speaks of culinary desserts
which are as thrilling an experience
as that which requires soft ancient slippers
before finally approaching table.

III
A constructed fence,
a new tenement,
the depth of life,
in blessed extreme,
a gathering of family.
Think images:
stakes of wood,
other possibilities:
entertainments to
lift the human spirit.

ORDINARY WORK

Because of my right club foot
the Government assigned me
a 4-F category and never
inducted me into any war we
fought. The physicians struggled
to straighten my right foot;
it is still $3^{1}/_{2}$ inches smaller
than my left foot. Still, I could have
kicked the shit out of any
enemy given the chance.
It was not so much the
principle of the thing;
it would have been
simply a matter of
life or death.

REGRET

Regret

For Charlotte

My great-aunt told this story with these words: *by the time I knew her, Marybelle was a fully grown woman and she was filled with the regret of human misery. She had begun her life by rejecting all of her previous suitors who came asking for her hand in matrimony. One of those men that she had rejected chose to stand at her door patiently, and after many years of lonely sorrow, she relented. Her womb produced three daughters while she sustained her husband's many rebukes. She was mired down in regret, so much so that she told me if she had the opportunity, she would reverse time, put her right foot on the breaks of her marriage and bring all of its activities to a screeching halt, back up completely out of the wedding dress, and step into that time which once signaled all kinds of possibilities for her womanly innocence. Could she reverse Destiny's Road with such a simple gesture? Was it possible to say no to the Rabbi and flee the synagogue with the pulse of life still beating in her small hands? Would God still support her actions? Or would he find her responsible and find some unsuspecting loophole and dole out a righteous punishment for her disobedience? I don't know what rightly happened to that young lady, but I'm guessing she either backed up out of that wedding dress or she died. Either way, she was no longer suffering, the way I see it.*

"... AND HE NEVER SAID A MUMBLING WORD,"

An African American Spiritual

The old man gathered together the fallen leaves,
shards of gossip, pieces of enlightenment about
his wife who had suffered an aneurysm which
exposed her physical capabilities to her neighbors
who only wanted to lend a hand of assistance.
Consider this not a failure of human attention.
The old man did not voice an opinion; he imparted
nothing which could be taken as new information.
He had absorbed the lessons of his thirty-year
marriage; no one had suggested anything other
than that marriage had been an adjustment.
His mother had warned that he would shit,
and step in it. He could not have guessed the
truth of her prediction. Stepping back,
the stench would last longer than the initial event.
The lingering odor would mark the moment.
He concentrated on the leaves before him,
gathering and raking them toward heaven.
Silence was the faith he kept with himself.
He repeated nothing that would cause
discomfort to his wife's presence. His mantra
became: this is what marriage is all about.

Kitchen Activity

An old woman sharpens her kitchen knives,
blue sparks from the implements like stars
around the room as if the ceiling was a cloud.

She slices the invasive sunlight into thin pieces;
she places them on a blue plate to be served with
tomatoes and mustard and healthy wheat bread.

The humid air is like the tread of a dinosaur
heavy and noisy. The old woman serves vegetables.
The room feels as if it is smothered in gravy.

Whenever a lonely man comes to the door,
he is invited in with devastatingly seductive whispers;
he is unable to resist the prepared cold cuts.

A quiet is stored in that house, frozen in the suburb of its heart.
There is a natural blue surrounding the old woman like a
     careless
negligee that ends up, in the late afternoon, on the kitchen floor.

CHAMPION

His kidneys were the boxing gloves
when Joe Louis contended
with Max Schmeling for the
Heavyweight Championship of the
World. They both had untold strength.
The black community listened
to the broadcast with uncompromising
quiet and cheered when the final bell
was rung on the radio.
They breathed a unified communal
sigh of congratulations;
they heralded that someone black
had defeated a white man fair and square,
somewhere in the world, and that they
would be able to rise and go to work
the next morning with a quiet pride
on their lips and suffer no
repercussions for this personal joy.

FISH STORY

Nobody condones absences;
the subway is a disco of
sexual energy pulsing its way
towards some incline or
cul de sac leading toward
purgatory, leaving behind
a photograph of its speed,
which takes me back to
wondering what is the
ethical thing to do about
lateness or absences?
A housewife spends her
days trying to cook up
reasons for lost time;
she is an express subway
trying to achieve a goal
with as few steps as possible.
Speed is an old world mosaic
taking us towards a special
ceremony, a colorful winter's
tale that suggests what
an evolutionary fish story
might sound like if it is told
in regards to our human heritage
whose days never seem to end.

UNTITLED #2

for: George R. Garrison
Who learned his craft in Buffalo,
enriched it in California, and
distributed it to the needy in Kent

A little old man, in a white scruffy beard,
comes towards me to inform me that my
shoelaces have come undone; he must
think that my life is unraveling strand by
strand before his very tense blue eyes;
he wants me to take better care of myself
and the possessions that I claim, because
everything before him is fleeting.
He seems willing to retie my shoes,
but I get the job done before he can say
Jackie Robinson! Instantly, my books fall
to the ground; I have to admit I will always
have trouble and always need help.
He quickly gathers up the splayed books,
arranges them smartly, and hands them
back to me respectfully.

Before the Kitchen Stove:
A Grandfather Addresses His Family
After the Death of His Wife

I am sitting in front of the kitchen stove; it has always been warmest here. I am putting all of you slow-assed individuals out of my house. You are thieves and you don't possess guns. You cannot be trusted. I am exhausted from making a way out of no way for all of you. I am locking the doors, pulling down the shades, and closing out my bank account. I am taking my ass on vacation to Hawaii or Europe or somewhere beside here, where you can't get in touch with me, and by the time I know you are in trouble, you will have solved your problems, or you will be locked away safely where I can't get to you, and I won't have to worry any more. You all have been trying to drive me crazy from the moment God introduced me to you. Today we buried your grandmother, and the minute we lowered that casket I knew I was done. The grave is no place for me; I knew that this afternoon. So, I am getting myself together and getting out of here while I still have the chance to save myself before anyone else has a chance to put their hands out begging for money. So, by the time you actually know where I am and write me asking for a loan, and by the time I write back saying no!, all of your problems will be solved, or they will have grown so large you will be in jail. What I desire is for you all to stand on your own two feet; that is what I require. You can help each other out for a change. Solve your own damn problems and let me get a little peace of mind. Anyway, I can't do it for you anymore. You have got to apply yourselves. Your grandmother is dead, and I have got to get you all on the right track and out of this house. Clearly, I am not in my right mind to do you one more favor. None of you know how to keep your word, and that is a fact. You borrow money, but you do not pay it back. So, I am informing you right now, your bills are going to bite you directly in the ass and they're going to make you mighty uncomfortable. No use you asking yourselves, under your breath, why am I being so mean? Grandma would never do such a thing. You are right; she wouldn't, but she is gone, and I am here, and I am doing this thing, because it is right and necessary. You are all lazy, and you have got to wake up, no more being bullied into action. I do not want to participate. I did what I could while your grandmother was alive to keep the peace, and Lord knows it took every ounce of energy I had to spare, but now, I tell you like the old spiritual goes: "Too late, too late, Master Jesus done took the key and gone home!" That means, for those of you too stupid to think, the gate of "gimmie" is shut, and no one is ever going to open that door again. It is time for all of you to march on out of that front door and get the hell away from here. I am putting up a sign in the front yard: **No Slackers Needed. No Free Advice. No more talking. Git! Scramb! I am done; no need to turn me over!**

JANET JACKSON'S NIPPLE

*"maybe coming of age in the American sensual
darkness never seeing an unsmudged nipple, an
uncensored vagina, has left me forever infected
with an unquenchable lust of the eye:"*

—"Old Man," C. K. Williams

Whatever digits constructed that fatal costume,
it was not song. It was the faulty rhythm of a
white hand sweeping across the black breast
of prime time when young innocent eyes are
unswervingly focused on the dance of that
pale blue screen, for young eyes are always
attuned and willing to gamble on improving
their seductive moves, wanting to accomplish
the outrageous without consequences, and to
do so in the open: something that their parents
had always warned against, even in the close
and unrevealing dark. Still, no parent would
admit to dispensing such acts of subservience
because of what they always had the good
sense to commit under cover. The guilty boy's
mother advised him handily: *Apologize quickly,
and your problems will disappear as quickly
as an extinguished klieg light.*

THE WARNING

The old grandmother recounted in a severe voice:
My great-granddaughter danced with the Devil.
I said: *Gal, don't you do that. It ain't right.*
But she did it anyway, and then, here she comes
crying like the foolish child she was.
I said: *What are you crying for? Now you are all*
spent and ain't going to be worth two cents to
anyone for the rest of your natural born life.
You made this mess and now you have to clean
it up or sleep in it. Those are your choices.
You see I have lived long enough
to see the Austrians do the same thing
and they called it "The Waltz."
I saw the Gypsies all over Europe do it
and they called it "The Tarantella."
People all over the world take chances,
but you have got to know what the hell you're doing.
I saw the freed slaves mix it up with the Devil,
and they called it "The Boogie-Woogie."
I have seen all sorts of peoples
dancing with Satan, and I know for a fact,
it don't pay no wages; it don't bring you no lasting glory,
cause I have lived my share of life on this earth, and it is
an expensive and costly act to dance with the Devil,
and mind you now, you spend a lifetime paying on
just the interest, and nobody ever, ever tells you
that it is the principal that you got to get down as well.
Look at how famous Michael became dancing his Moonwalk,
and all the little mannish black and white boys followed him
like he was the Pied Piper of Hamlin doing what they called
  "Breakdancing."

I know all of this for a clear fact, for you see, I am an old-timer;
a seer, who has spent some quality time dancing with the Devil
  too.
So, I know what it is I am talking about!

Hands
of
Imagination

A Dusting of Snow

Tender snow
salutes the empty trees,
the funeral crows,
swift swallows gliding
effortlessly on wings,
in lock step
blank as a washed
beach that is touched by
sunlight and vigorous winds
quickly dispelling those
pale shadows that linger
after a burial on a cold
Monday morning.

OUTSIDE THE GATE

I no longer hope to get into heaven.
I want a chair placed outside the gate;
that will do;
that will do.
Only the simple dead attain heaven.
Do not ask how I know this;
their activity is their just reward.
A chair will do me just fine.
I do not seek the comfort of heaven.
The dead will receive their promise,
one by one, as a carriage drives them
into rest.

If the good you accomplished was not purposeful
and a generous amount of what you did was bad,
then you are left hopeless and sad.
So, you see why a simple chair will do me fine,
since I leave no purposeful good behind.
There are many who still seek lasting eternity;
I simply seek a reserved chair
placed comfortably outside the gate.
I promise not to arrive late.

Short Poem

The windows of the soul
the sullen light appears to be the blame:
uncolored, unadorned, unrestrained.
There are no miracles of grace abounding,
there is nothing, nothing which shunts
or shuns the senses.
Nothing.

THE WAR DEAD

Solemnly, the right foot salutes the air;
the left foot holds firmly to the ground.
Six British soldiers shoulder a nation's grief;
their march invokes a solemn wound.

A widow stands in her wooden doorway waiting;
she is a stature of mournful greeting at the door;
she is dressed in appropriate black;
she will not celebrate life anymore.

Six soldiers' left feet swivel in the air;
their right feet grasp the sacred ground.
Six soldiers bear the coffin forward;
their feet, in hushed tones, make little sound.

Of the six humbled British soldiers
only three are seen in stark relief:
their cheeks embrace a side of the coffin,
they whisper a song about war's endless grief.

In the Jungles of South America

blind inland waterways
piranhas eat their days.
they swim from feasting.
the surface water holds
the scraps of their leavings;
hunger has been assuaged;
silence listens to what
the jungle has to say.

Out Back

The wind sweeps through the deepest parts of the woods behind our house where the lands begins to sink in rot. We never venture beyond that point; it is not entirely safe to do so. We know that there are deer residing in those unsafe regions during the long winters we suffer through, where the subject of how they keep warm comes up. We do not have any radical answers on how they forage for food, where they sleep or how they procreate, but they do because the species seem alive and well when we see them walking casually through the leftover debris of winter. Something takes place in what has become a reserve, but rest assured, I cannot inform you with any certainty or with one single iota of evidence about what it is that takes place.

Standing Beneath Grapes

ripe with sensuous liquor,
a moon of iridescent fruit,
a Sanskrit Tree marks the dust.
Dogs give over to Armageddon;
the giraffe grows taller
ashamed of its height,
reaching for the unattainable,
a steel skeleton in the air.
No athlete can lift such fruit:
it withdraws from human touch,
even the air cannot hold its weight.
Nothing may touch those grapes,
not human hands nor ravenous teeth
which suggests a richness may spill
from these fruits into human palms
brimming with luscious weight;
these grapes fall under their own command;
curses being the implements of gods
lightening their weapon of choice,
while a spear of retribution or
an old-fashioned plow may only
alter the roots of things.

CELEBRATING THE DECADES

When the aging professor entered into his seventh decade
he still read the daily obituaries to see if he
encountered his name. He took note of the dearly
departed especially those that he knew, and loved, and those
who were the less fortunate, whose names meant they were
his contemporaries. He had always tried to enjoy the labors
that others produced. He had lost all of his natural teeth and
had replaced them with a false smile. He was hard-pressed
to find something good to smile about. His life was a
constant struggle to push his lawn mower back and forth;
the terrain of his yard was rough, it contained small
mountains, and lonely valleys. His neighbors were
swifter because they were younger. Their children screamed
satisfaction, their joys were outrageous. They were not
conditioned to face human disappointments. He predicted
that they would live awhile and then arrive at junctures
of immediacy and announce to everyone within earshot
that they were fully prepared, but nothing of the
sort would be true.

CODA

A Faulty Sonnet

Pick, ax, wire, rake, one farmer goes farther;
he had never wanted to journey hither and thither.

That day, an immigrant, a devout grandfather
plowed a stream that rubbed itself into a deeper
gully; trying to restrain it from gnawing a singular
path that would divide the land, he plowed each acre.

All of his muscles, loosely hung on his bones,
made warmth for his house, an achieved spirit,
a wood of freedom, a righteous space for ones
that he loved and celebrated by sensing it,

and seeing it as a struggle laced with determination,
a teaching of how to keep close to the earth. Slowly
he reaps posterity from the wind-dust of his station,
the bliss of women, and the seasons of disparity.

Unknown

In memory of William Paul Baron

are those mysterious words,
a tangle of meaning,
spoken by the Rabbi,
intoned by the Creator.
Neither bring results;
nothing is secured
with spit and glue, mortar
or bailing wire.
What saves us love
is a word that's
spoken or sung,
a thought beyond apology
that engenders in the air
and results from a breath
that comes from somewhere
unknown.

A SONNET FOR JUDITH

for Judith Baron LaValle

Write me a poem that I can understand,
where the secrets you share are only for me,
for water is destructive, and so is sand.
I want to be privy to all that you can see.

All knowledge regurgitates toward the sea,
and recognizes that exact shade of truth
and buries old habits for centuries,
for the house we live in must have a roof.

Let us abandon the moon, its spirit,
its movable soul which can be identified
as skin and blood and bones that sometimes cry,
but will never lie; but will never lie.

This song is for me and only me;
I will not share it with the wind or sea.

Villanelle for an Auspicious Occasion

To the sacred memory of Abraham Lincoln

He gave our fathers and mothers a reason to offer life as an
inheritance
the stringencies of their time taught them to look at each other
in the eye;
hope is what provided them with the materials for work and
dance.

The nameless men and women who went to war, with clear
assurance,
who had in their possession a notion of what freedom was,
breathed a daring sign.
They were the destined mothers and fathers who fortified our
sure inheritance.

The inevitability of those political days has defined the future of
our existence;
that was right, and just, and true; now, we have little cause to
question why.
Hope is what provides us with all the materials for work and
dance.

We see eye to eye, we stand shoulder to shoulder with a
determined stance.
We shall preserve the wealth of this nation for all those destined
to live or die;
that is what our fathers and mothers provided for us as a rightful
inheritance.

We here, then, dedicate with pure purpose this sweet cause to
enhance
what Lincoln, with generous justice, did while he stood and
braved the
laudatory heights to carve out a destiny for our country. In work
and dance

Lincoln still gives light to this very day; let it define our joyous
existence,
let it state who we are, and what we have become, since history
dare not lie.
This gift is what our fathers and mothers gave, rendering it a
worthy inheritance,
through the valuable materials of hope and work, for love and
for the dance.

A Villanelle for the End of 2013

I look at all of the animal objects which are made
and am glad I am part of the process:
a craftsman, who can fashion Chinese jade,

an Egyptian mystic who has, stone on stone, laid
pyramids in the sun's perfect symmetry with ease.
I willingly entertain objects which have been made

like the Taj Mahal in an alabaster shade,
the Brooklyn Bridge which waits for man to sneeze,
like the craftsmen who can easily fashion jade.

These are men of achievement, not only of shade
or light alone, but made to hug and squeeze
and consider those things which are naturally made:

the stunning mountains, the streams, the vast glades
of dark wildernesses, where men work to please
like those craftsmen whose bodies never wheezed

holding naked jewels in hand that did not seem staid
nor breakable at the slightest or single sneeze.
So, I look at all objects which are made
like those craftsmen who once fashioned Chinese jade.

CPSIA information can be obtained
at www.ICGtesting.com
Printed in the USA
FFHW020559220819
54371198-60090FF